Taking Charge of Your Low Blood Pressure

A Guide to Feeling Your Best

Aria Vitality

DEDICATION

To all those who strive for inner peace, balance, and well-being amidst life's myriad challenges. Your courage, resilience, and commitment to personal growth inspire the pages of this book. May these words serve as a guiding light on your journey towards a harmonious and fulfilled life.

CONTENTS

ACKNOWLEDGMENTS

This book is the culmination of collective wisdom, support, and encouragement from numerous individuals and resources. I extend my deepest gratitude to all those who have contributed to its creation.

To my family and friends, thank you for your unwavering love, patience, and understanding throughout this endeavor. Your support has been my anchor during moments of doubt and inspiration during times of creativity.

I am indebted to the mental health professionals whose expertise and dedication have shaped the content of this book. Your commitment to helping others navigate the complexities of the mind is truly commendable.

To the readers who embark on this journey of self-discovery and growth, thank you for entrusting me with your time and attention. It is my sincere hope that the insights shared within these pages resonate with you and empower you to cultivate a life of balance, resilience, and fulfillment.

Finally, I extend my heartfelt appreciation to the team at SmartWave Research Group, whose professionalism, guidance, and enthusiasm have brought this project to fruition.

With deep appreciation,
Aria Vitality

CHAPTER 1

Understanding Low Blood Pressure

Blood pressure, the force exerted by circulating blood against your artery walls, plays a critical role in transporting oxygen and nutrients throughout your body. This chapter delves into the world of low blood pressure, also known as hypotension, explaining what it is, what constitutes normal readings, how it's measured, and why it matters for your overall health.

1.1 What is Low Blood Pressure (Hypotension)?

Low blood pressure, medically termed hypotension, refers to a condition where the force of blood flowing through your arteries is consistently lower than the recommended range for your age and health status. This reduced pressure can impact the ability of your blood to deliver vital oxygen and nutrients to your organs and tissues, potentially leading to a variety of symptoms.

There are two main classifications of low blood pressure:

- **Primary (Chronic) Hypotension:** This type occurs for no apparent underlying cause. It's often present for a long time and may not worsen significantly. It's more common in young adults and can sometimes be associated with dehydration, certain medications, or prolonged bed rest.

- **Secondary (Acute) Hypotension:** This type arises due to a specific medical condition, medication, or situation. It can be sudden and severe, requiring prompt medical attention. Causes of secondary hypotension can include dehydration (especially in older adults or people with chronic illnesses), blood loss (due to injury, surgery, or internal bleeding), severe infections (sepsis), allergic reactions (anaphylaxis), heart problems (heart failure, arrhythmias), and certain medications (diuretics, vasodilators, some antidepressants).

It's important to note that the specific symptoms you experience with low blood pressure can vary depending on the severity of the condition and any underlying causes.

1.2 Normal Blood Pressure Readings

Understanding what constitutes "normal" blood pressure is crucial for interpreting your readings and identifying potential issues. Blood pressure readings are written as two numbers separated by a slash. The top number, **systolic pressure**, represents the pressure exerted when your heart contracts and pushes blood out. The bottom number, **diastolic pressure**, reflects the pressure between heartbeats when your heart relaxes and refills with blood.

The American Heart Association (AHA) categorizes blood pressure readings as follows (**keep in mind these are general guidelines**):

- **Normal:** Less than 120/80 mmHg (millimeters of

mercury)

- **Elevated:** Systolic between 120-129 mmHg and diastolic less than 80 mmHg

- **Stage 1 Hypertension:** Systolic between 130-139 mmHg or diastolic between 80-89 mmHg

- **Stage 2 Hypertension:** Systolic at least 140 mmHg or diastolic at least 90 mmHg

Age Considerations: As you age, your arteries naturally become stiffer, which can lead to slightly higher blood pressure readings. Your doctor will determine your ideal blood pressure range based on your age, overall health, and any existing medical conditions. It's important to discuss your blood pressure readings with your doctor to understand if they fall within a healthy range for you.

Here are some additional factors that can influence blood pressure readings:

- **Time of Day:** Blood pressure tends to be naturally lower at night and higher in the morning.

- **Activity Level:** Blood pressure typically rises during physical activity and then returns to baseline levels when you're resting.

- **Stress:** Emotional stress can cause temporary spikes in blood pressure.

- **Diet:** A diet high in sodium (salt) can contribute to high blood pressure, while a healthy diet rich in fruits, vegetables, and whole grains can help maintain healthy blood pressure levels.

1.3 How is Blood Pressure Measured?

Measuring blood pressure is a simple and painless procedure typically performed by a doctor, nurse, or other healthcare professional. Here's what to expect:

- **Preparation:** You'll be asked to rest comfortably for a few minutes before the measurement. Avoid smoking, caffeine, and exercise for at least 30 minutes beforehand, as these can elevate your readings. Empty your bladder if needed, as a full bladder can slightly raise your blood pressure.

- **The Equipment:** A sphygmomanometer is used, consisting of an inflatable cuff wrapped around your upper arm and a stethoscope placed over your brachial artery at the elbow. There are also digital blood pressure monitors available for home use.

- **The Process:** The cuff is inflated until blood flow is blocked, then slowly released. The doctor will listen for sounds through the stethoscope, which correspond to blood flow returning through the artery. These sounds are used to determine your systolic and diastolic pressure.

- **Multiple Readings:** It's common to take multiple readings throughout a single visit or over several visits to get a more accurate picture of your overall blood pressure. This is because blood pressure can naturally fluctuate throughout the day depending on various factors. Your doctor may also take readings on both arms to ensure there are no significant discrepancies.

Home Blood Pressure Monitoring: While not a substitute for professional medical advice, home blood pressure monitors can be a valuable tool for tracking your blood pressure readings between doctor visits. These monitors are readily available at most pharmacies and drugstores. However, it's crucial to choose a validated device and follow the manufacturer's instructions for proper use.

Here are some additional tips for accurate home blood pressure monitoring:

1. Sit comfortably with your back supported and your feet flat on the floor.
2. Rest for at least 5 minutes before taking a reading.
3. Use the upper arm cuff on the bare arm, not over clothing.
4. Ensure the cuff is positioned correctly and feels snug but not uncomfortable.
5. Avoid talking or moving while the measurement is being taken.
6. Record your readings, including the date, time, and any relevant notes about your activity level or how

you're feeling.

7. Discuss your home readings with your doctor to understand their significance in the context of your overall health.

When to See a Doctor About Blood Pressure Readings:

It's important to consult your doctor if:

1. You experience any persistent symptoms that might be related to low blood pressure, such as dizziness, lightheadedness, fatigue, or fainting.
2. Your home blood pressure readings are consistently outside the normal range, even if you don't have any symptoms.
3. You have a pre-existing medical condition that can affect blood pressure, such as heart disease, diabetes, or kidney disease.

1.4 Why is Blood Pressure Important?

Blood pressure is vital for ensuring proper blood flow throughout your body. Adequate blood pressure delivers oxygen and nutrients to your organs and tissues, allowing them to function correctly. When blood pressure drops too low, your body struggles to deliver these essential elements, leading to various problems.

Here's a breakdown of why maintaining healthy blood pressure is crucial:

- **Supplies Oxygen and Nutrients:** Blood carries oxygen and nutrients to all parts of your body. Low blood pressure can lead to inadequate oxygen delivery, potentially causing organ damage, fatigue, and impaired brain function.

- **Removes Waste Products:** Blood also transports waste products away from cells. With low blood pressure, this process can be hampered, leading to a buildup of toxins in the body.

- **Maintains Body Functions:** Organs like your kidneys, heart, and brain rely on proper blood pressure to function optimally. Low blood pressure can disrupt these functions, potentially leading to serious health complications.

- **Long-Term Consequences:** Chronically low blood pressure, even if not causing immediate symptoms, can contribute to long-term health problems like heart failure, stroke, and kidney disease.

Understanding low blood pressure equips you to recognize its signs and symptoms and seek timely medical attention if needed.

CHAPTER 2

While low blood pressure (hypotension) doesn't always cause noticeable symptoms, it can sometimes manifest in various ways depending on the severity of the condition and how quickly it develops. This chapter explores the common and less common symptoms associated with low blood pressure, helping you recognize potential issues and understand when to seek medical attention.

2.1 Common Symptoms

These are the most frequent symptoms you might experience with low blood pressure:

- **Dizziness and Lightheadedness:** This sensation of feeling woozy or unsteady is a classic sign of low blood pressure. It occurs because the brain isn't receiving enough oxygen-rich blood, leading to feelings of disorientation and possible imbalance.

- **Fatigue and Weakness:** When your body struggles to deliver oxygen and nutrients to your muscles and tissues due to low blood pressure, you might experience general fatigue and a lack of energy. This can make even routine activities feel more tiring.

- **Nausea and Vomiting:** In some cases, low blood pressure can disrupt your digestive system, leading to nausea and even vomiting. This is because the reduced blood flow can affect the proper functioning of your stomach and intestines.

- **Blurred Vision:** When your brain isn't receiving enough oxygenated blood, your vision can become blurry or dimmed. This symptom is usually temporary and resolves once your blood pressure returns to normal levels.

It's important to note that these symptoms can also be

caused by other underlying medical conditions. If you experience any of these symptoms frequently or with significant intensity, consult your doctor for a proper diagnosis.

2.2 Less Common Symptoms

While less frequent, some additional symptoms can sometimes occur with low blood pressure:

- **Difficulty Concentrating:** The reduced blood flow to your brain due to low blood pressure can affect cognitive function, making it harder to focus and concentrate. You might experience difficulty with tasks requiring mental clarity or memory.

- **Cold and Clammy Skin:** When your body tries to compensate for low blood pressure, it may constrict blood vessels in your skin to redirect blood flow to vital organs. This can lead to cold and clammy skin, especially in your hands and feet.

- **Rapid Breathing (Tachypnea):** Your body may try

to increase oxygen intake to compensate for the reduced blood flow with low pressure. This can manifest as rapid, shallow breathing.

- **Fainting (Syncope):** In severe cases of low blood pressure, particularly when it develops rapidly, fainting (syncope) can occur. This happens when there's not enough blood flow to the brain, causing temporary loss of consciousness. If you experience fainting spells, especially without warning, seek immediate medical attention.

Remember: The severity and combination of symptoms you experience can vary depending on the cause and severity of your low blood pressure. It's crucial to pay attention to your body and consult your doctor if you experience any persistent or concerning symptoms.

Additional Considerations:

- **Age:** Older adults are more susceptible to experiencing symptoms with low blood pressure, as their blood pressure regulation mechanisms might be less efficient.

- **Dehydration:** Dehydration can contribute to low blood pressure, and symptoms like dizziness and lightheadedness can worsen when dehydrated.

- **Underlying Conditions:** Certain medical conditions, such as diabetes, heart disease, and neurological disorders, can increase the risk of low blood pressure and its associated symptoms.

By understanding the potential symptoms of low blood pressure, you can be more proactive in monitoring your health and seeking medical attention when necessary. The following chapters will delve deeper into the causes, diagnosis, treatment options, and management strategies for low blood pressure, empowering you to maintain optimal health.

CHAPTER 3

Understanding the root cause of your low blood pressure (hypotension) is crucial for determining the appropriate treatment approach. This chapter explores the two main categories of low blood pressure - primary (chronic) and secondary (acute) - and delves into the various factors that can contribute to each type.

3.1 Primary (Chronic) Hypotension

Primary hypotension, also known as essential hypotension, occurs when there's no identifiable underlying medical condition causing the low blood pressure. It's often a long-term condition and may not worsen significantly over time. Here are the main subtypes of primary hypotension:

3.1.1 Idiopathic Hypotension (Unknown Cause): In

some cases, even after thorough medical evaluation, the exact reason for primary hypotension remains unclear. This is termed idiopathic hypotension.

3.1.2 Neurally Mediated Hypotension (Problems with Nervous System Control):

This type arises when the nervous system, particularly the autonomic nervous system, malfunctions in regulating blood pressure. The autonomic nervous system controls functions like heart rate and blood vessel constriction/dilation. In neurally mediated hypotension, the nervous system might not respond appropriately to changes in body position (like standing from sitting) or other stimuli, leading to a drop in blood pressure.

- **Orthostatic Hypotension:** This is the most common form of neurally mediated hypotension. It's characterized by a sudden drop in blood pressure when changing positions, particularly from lying down or sitting to standing. This can cause dizziness, lightheadedness, and even fainting. It's more prevalent in young adults and older adults alike.

- **Postprandial Hypotension:** This subtype occurs after meals, particularly large meals high in carbohydrates. The blood flow gets diverted to the digestive system for food processing, causing a temporary dip in blood pressure to other parts of the body. This can lead to symptoms like dizziness and fatigue after eating.

3.1.3 Endocrine Hypotension (Hormonal Imbalances):

Certain hormonal imbalances can contribute to primary hypotension. For example, a deficiency in adrenal hormones, which help regulate blood pressure, can lead to low blood pressure.

3.2 Secondary (Acute) Hypotension

Secondary hypotension arises due to a specific medical condition, medication, or situation. It can be sudden and severe, requiring prompt medical attention. Here are some common causes of secondary hypotension:

3.2.1 Dehydration: When your body doesn't have enough fluids, the volume of blood circulating through your system decreases. This reduced blood volume can lead to a drop in blood pressure. Dehydration can occur due to insufficient fluid intake, excessive sweating, vomiting, or diarrhea.

3.2.2 Blood Loss: Significant blood loss from an injury, surgery, or internal bleeding can cause a rapid decrease in blood volume, leading to severe hypotension. This is a medical emergency requiring immediate treatment.

3.2.3 Medications: Certain medications, such as diuretics used for high blood pressure, vasodilators that widen blood vessels, and some antidepressants, can have a side effect of lowering blood pressure. It's crucial to discuss potential side effects with your doctor and understand how your medications might affect your blood pressure.

3.2.4 Infections: Severe infections, also known as sepsis, can trigger widespread inflammation in the body, leading to vasodilation (widening of blood vessels) and a subsequent drop in blood pressure. This can be a life-threatening condition requiring prompt medical intervention.

Additional Considerations:

- **Certain Medical Conditions:** Underlying medical conditions like heart disease, heart failure, diabetes, and neurological disorders can contribute to secondary hypotension. These conditions can affect the heart's ability to pump blood effectively or disrupt the nervous system's role in blood pressure regulation.

- **Anaphylaxis:** A severe allergic reaction called anaphylaxis can cause a sudden drop in blood pressure due to widespread vasodilation and fluid leakage from blood vessels. It's a medical emergency requiring immediate medical attention.

Knowing the various causes of low blood pressure empowers you to identify potential triggers and take preventive measures.

CHAPTER 4

RISK FACTORS FOR LOW BLOOD PRESSURE

While anyone can experience low blood pressure (hypotension) occasionally, certain factors can increase your susceptibility. Understanding these risk factors empowers you to take proactive steps to maintain healthy blood pressure and reduce your chances of complications. This chapter explores the various elements that can contribute to the development of low blood pressure.

4.1 Age

Age is a significant risk factor for low blood pressure. Here's how it plays a role:

- **Arterial Stiffness:** As you age, your arteries naturally become stiffer and less elastic. This can make it harder for blood to flow efficiently, potentially leading to slightly higher blood pressure readings. However, in some older adults, the body's ability to regulate blood pressure might become less effective, leading to dips in blood pressure instead.

- **Orthostatic Hypotension:** This form of low blood pressure that occurs upon standing is more common in older adults. This is because the body's mechanisms for adjusting blood pressure to postural changes (like standing from sitting) might become less efficient with age.

- **Dehydration:** Older adults are generally more susceptible to dehydration, which can contribute to low blood pressure. Reduced fluid intake due to medications or age-related changes in thirst sensation can be factors.

It's important to note that not all older adults experience low blood pressure. However, being aware of the increased risk allows for closer monitoring and earlier intervention if needed.

4.2 Certain Medications

Some medications can have a side effect of lowering blood pressure. Here are some common examples:

- **Diuretics:** These medications are used to treat high blood pressure and heart failure by helping the body remove excess fluid through urination. While effective for their intended purpose, diuretics can also lead to low blood pressure, especially if not taken as prescribed or combined with other blood pressure-lowering medications.

- **Vasodilators:** These medications widen blood vessels, which can be helpful for treating conditions like angina (chest pain) or heart failure. However, vasodilators can also lead to a drop in blood pressure, particularly when taken at high doses.

- **Antidepressants:** Some types of antidepressants, particularly tricyclic antidepressants, can have a side effect of lowering blood pressure. It's crucial to discuss potential side effects with your doctor and understand how your medications might affect your blood pressure.

If you take any medications, it's important to be aware of their potential side effects and discuss any concerns with your doctor. They can adjust your medication dosage or switch you to a different medication if necessary to minimize the risk of low blood pressure.

4.3 Dehydration

Dehydration occurs when your body loses more fluids than it takes in. This can happen due to insufficient fluid intake, excessive sweating (particularly in hot weather or during exercise), vomiting, or diarrhea. When dehydrated, the volume of blood circulating through your system decreases, leading to a drop in blood pressure. Dehydration can worsen pre-existing low blood pressure or trigger it in individuals who are otherwise healthy.

Here are some tips to stay hydrated and prevent dehydration-related low blood pressure:

- Drink plenty of fluids throughout the day, even if you don't feel thirsty. Aim for water as your primary beverage, but unsweetened teas and low-fat milk can also contribute to hydration.

- Be mindful of your fluid needs during hot weather or exercise, as you lose fluids more readily through sweating. Increase your fluid intake accordingly.

- If you experience vomiting or diarrhea, replenish fluids with water or electrolyte-rich beverages to prevent dehydration.

4.4 Underlying Medical Conditions

Certain medical conditions can contribute to low blood pressure. Here's a closer look at some common culprits:

4.4.1 Heart Disease: Conditions that weaken the heart muscle or affect its pumping ability can lead to low blood pressure. This is because the heart can't pump blood as effectively, leading to reduced blood flow and pressure. Examples include heart failure, arrhythmias (irregular heartbeats), and valvular heart disease.

4.4.2 Diabetes: Uncontrolled diabetes can damage nerves that control blood pressure regulation, potentially leading to low blood pressure, especially upon standing.

4.4.3 Neurological Disorders: Conditions like Parkinson's disease and autonomic neuropathy (damage to nerves that control involuntary body functions) can disrupt the nervous system's role in blood pressure regulation, contributing to low blood pressure.

Early diagnosis and management of these underlying medical conditions are crucial to prevent complications, including low blood pressure.

4.5 Pregnancy

Pregnancy is a unique situation that can affect blood

pressure. While some women experience no significant changes, others might develop postural hypotension (low blood pressure upon standing) during pregnancy. This is because the growing uterus can compress blood vessels in the abdomen, reducing blood flow back to the heart and potentially leading to a drop in blood.

- **Blood Volume Expansion:** During pregnancy, your blood volume naturally increases to support the developing baby. However, this expansion can sometimes outpace the increase in blood pressure resistance, leading to a slight decrease in blood pressure, particularly in the second trimester. This is usually not a cause for concern unless accompanied by symptoms.

- **Hormonal Changes:** Pregnancy hormones like progesterone can cause blood vessels to relax, contributing to lower blood pressure.

It's important to note that low blood pressure during pregnancy can sometimes be a sign of an underlying medical condition, such as preeclampsia. Preeclampsia is a serious pregnancy complication characterized by high blood pressure and signs of damage to other organ systems. If you experience any concerning symptoms like severe dizziness, vision changes, or persistent headaches during pregnancy, consult your doctor immediately.

Additional Risk Factors:

- **Anemia:** A lack of red blood cells, which carry oxygen throughout the body, can contribute to low blood pressure. This is because there are fewer red blood cells available to transport oxygen, and the body might compensate by lowering blood pressure.

- **Vitamin Deficiencies:** Deficiencies in certain vitamins, particularly vitamin B12, can affect the nervous system and potentially disrupt blood pressure regulation.

- **Bed Rest:** Prolonged periods of bed rest can lead to a decrease in blood pressure. This is because bed rest can cause a decrease in blood volume and a decline in muscle tone, both of which can contribute to lower blood pressure.

Other Considerations:

- **Certain medical conditions** like eating disorders or severe allergic reactions (anaphylaxis) can also contribute to low blood pressure.

- **Lifestyle factors** such as excessive alcohol consumption or use of recreational drugs can also increase your risk of low blood pressure.

By understanding the various risk factors for low blood pressure, you can be more proactive in maintaining healthy blood pressure and minimizing your risk of complications.

CHAPTER 5

While low blood pressure (hypotension) doesn't always cause noticeable symptoms, it can sometimes lead to serious complications if left untreated. This chapter explores the potential consequences of chronically low blood pressure, emphasizing the importance of early diagnosis and management.

5.1 Falls and Injuries

One of the most common complications of low blood pressure is an increased risk of falls and injuries. Here's why:

- **Dizziness and Lightheadedness:** These common symptoms of low blood pressure can cause sudden feelings of disorientation and instability, making you more prone to tripping or losing your balance. This can lead to falls, especially in older adults or people with mobility limitations.

- **Reduced Blood Flow to the Brain:** When blood pressure drops, the brain receives less oxygen-rich blood. This can lead to temporary episodes of lightheadedness or dizziness, further increasing the risk of falls.

Preventing Falls:

- **Maintaining good balance and strength** through regular exercise can help prevent falls.

- **Ensuring proper home safety measures** like installing grab bars in bathrooms and removing tripping hazards can minimize fall risks.

- **Wearing well-fitting shoes** with good traction provides better stability when walking.

- **Discussing your fall risk** with your doctor and getting appropriate recommendations can help prevent falls and potential injuries.

5.2 Organ Damage (Brain, Kidneys)

Chronically low blood pressure can have detrimental effects on vital organs if left unchecked. Here's a closer look:

- **Brain:** When the brain doesn't receive enough oxygen-rich blood due to low blood pressure, it can lead to cognitive decline, memory problems, and difficulty concentrating. In severe cases, low blood pressure can contribute to ministrokes or transient ischemic attacks (TIAs), which are temporary blockages of blood flow to the brain that can cause temporary neurological symptoms.

- **Kidneys:** The kidneys rely on adequate blood flow to function properly and filter waste products from the blood. Chronically low blood pressure can impair kidney function and potentially lead to kidney damage over time.

Early diagnosis and treatment of low blood pressure are

crucial to prevent these complications and ensure proper blood flow to vital organs.

5.3 Cognitive Decline

As mentioned earlier, chronically low blood pressure can negatively impact cognitive function. Here's a breakdown of the potential consequences:

- **Reduced Blood Flow to the Brain:** As discussed previously, low blood pressure reduces the brain's supply of oxygen-rich blood. This can lead to difficulty concentrating, memory problems, and slower thinking.

- **Silent Damage:** In some cases, low blood pressure might not cause noticeable symptoms initially, but it can silently damage brain tissue over time. This can contribute to a gradual decline in cognitive function and increase the risk of dementia in older adults.

Maintaining Healthy Blood Pressure throughout your

life is crucial for promoting optimal cognitive health and reducing the risk of age-related cognitive decline.

5.4 Increased Risk of Death (Severe Cases)

In severe cases, particularly when low blood pressure develops rapidly due to significant blood loss, severe infection, or allergic reaction (anaphylaxis), it can be life-threatening. This is because organs like the brain, heart, and kidneys rely on adequate blood flow to function. When blood pressure drops significantly, these organs become deprived of oxygen and nutrients, which can lead to organ failure and death if not treated promptly.

Early intervention is critical in such situations. If you experience severe symptoms like fainting, confusion, or difficulty breathing, seek immediate medical attention.

Remember: Early diagnosis and treatment of low blood pressure are essential to prevent complications and ensure optimal health.

CHAPTER 6

An accurate diagnosis of low blood pressure (hypotension) is crucial for determining the underlying cause and implementing the most effective treatment approach. This chapter explores the various methods healthcare professionals use to diagnose low blood pressure and identify any potential contributing factors.

6.1 Medical History and Physical Examination

The diagnostic process typically begins with a comprehensive medical history and physical examination by your doctor. Here's what you can expect:

- **Medical History:** Your doctor will ask detailed questions about your current symptoms, including their frequency, severity, and any situations that

36

trigger them. They will also inquire about your past medical history, any medications you take, and lifestyle habits like smoking or alcohol consumption.

- **Physical Examination:** During the physical exam, your doctor will measure your blood pressure in both arms while you're lying down, sitting, and standing. Checking blood pressure in different positions helps identify postural hypotension, which is a specific type that occurs upon standing. Your doctor will also listen to your heart and lungs for any abnormalities and assess your overall health.

Based on the information gathered, your doctor might determine that a simple blood pressure measurement and physical examination are sufficient for diagnosis, especially if your symptoms are mild and there are no underlying medical conditions. However, in some cases, further testing might be necessary.

6.2 Blood Pressure Measurement Techniques

Accurate blood pressure measurement is essential for diagnosing low blood pressure. Here's an overview of the techniques used:

- **Standard Sphygmomanometer:** This is the traditional method, using an inflatable cuff wrapped around your upper arm and a stethoscope to listen for sounds as the cuff pressure is gradually released.

- **Automatic Blood Pressure Monitors:** These electronic devices offer a convenient way to measure blood pressure at home. However, it's crucial to choose a validated device and use it properly according to the manufacturer's instructions. Home blood pressure monitoring can be a valuable tool for tracking your blood pressure trends between doctor visits, but it shouldn't replace regular professional checkups.

Multiple Blood Pressure Readings: A single blood pressure reading might not be entirely representative of your overall blood pressure health. Your doctor might take several readings throughout a single visit or recommend monitoring your blood pressure at home over a period to get a more accurate picture.

6.3 Additional Tests

Depending on your individual situation and the doctor's findings from the initial evaluation, additional tests might be recommended to identify the underlying cause of your low blood pressure. Here are some examples:

6.3.1 Blood Tests: Blood tests can help assess your overall health, identify potential underlying conditions like anemia or vitamin deficiencies that might contribute to low blood pressure, and evaluate your kidney function, as low blood pressure can sometimes affect kidney health.

6.3.2 Electrocardiogram (ECG): An ECG is a painless test that measures the electrical activity of your heart. It can help detect heart rhythm problems (arrhythmias) that might be contributing to low blood pressure.

6.3.3 Tilt-Table Test: This test is used specifically to diagnose neurally mediated hypotension, particularly postural hypotension. During the test, you'll be positioned on a table that's tilted to different angles, simulating changes in body position. Your blood pressure and heart rate are monitored throughout the test to see if they drop significantly when you move from a lying down to a standing position.

The specific tests your doctor recommends will depend on your individual circumstances and suspected cause of your low blood pressure. Early diagnosis and identification of any underlying conditions are crucial for effective treatment and preventing potential complications.

CHAPTER 7

TREATMENT FOR LOW BLOOD PRESSURE

Fortunately, low blood pressure (hypotension) can often be managed effectively with a combination of lifestyle modifications and, in some cases, medications. This chapter explores the various treatment options available to help you maintain healthy blood pressure and improve your overall well-being.

7.1 Lifestyle Modifications

Lifestyle modifications are often the first line of defense in managing low blood pressure. These changes can be highly effective, particularly for cases of primary (chronic) hypotension or mild secondary (acute) hypotension. Here are some key strategies:

7.1.1 Increased Fluid Intake: Dehydration is a common

contributor to low blood pressure. Increasing your fluid intake throughout the day can help to increase blood volume and improve blood pressure. Aim for water as your primary beverage, but unsweetened teas, low-fat milk, and diluted fruit juices can also contribute to hydration.

Here are some tips for staying hydrated:

- Carry a reusable water bottle with you and sip on it throughout the day.

- Set reminders on your phone or use a hydration app to encourage yourself to drink regularly.

- Eat plenty of fruits and vegetables, which also have a high water content.

- Be mindful of your fluid needs during hot weather or exercise, as you lose fluids more readily through sweating. Increase your fluid intake accordingly.

7.1.2 Dietary Changes (Salt Increase): It's important to note that consulting with your doctor before significantly increasing your salt intake is crucial. For people with low blood pressure who are not on a salt-restricted diet for other medical conditions (like heart disease or high blood pressure), a moderate increase in dietary salt (sodium) can be helpful. Sodium helps retain fluids in the body, which can increase blood volume and improve blood pressure. However, excessive salt intake can be detrimental to overall health, so moderation is key. Discuss appropriate sodium intake levels with your doctor based on your individual needs.

In addition to potentially increasing salt intake, here are some other dietary recommendations that may be beneficial:

- Eat a balanced diet rich in fruits, vegetables, and whole grains. These foods are packed with essential nutrients that can support overall health and potentially improve blood pressure regulation.

- Limit processed foods, sugary drinks, and unhealthy fats, which can contribute to various health problems, including those affecting blood pressure.

7.1.3 Compression Stockings: Compression stockings are elastic stockings that apply gentle pressure to your legs. This can help improve blood flow from your legs back to your heart, potentially leading to a slight increase in blood pressure. Compression stockings are most effective for people with postural hypotension, where blood pressure drops significantly upon standing.

7.1.4 Exercise Strategies: Regular exercise can be a powerful tool for managing low blood pressure. Exercise helps improve heart function, blood flow, and overall circulation. However, it's crucial to start slowly and gradually increase the intensity and duration of your workouts as your fitness improves. Discuss appropriate exercise routines with your doctor, especially if you have any underlying health conditions.

Here are some exercise tips for individuals with low blood pressure:

- Engage in regular aerobic activities like brisk

walking, swimming, or cycling. Aim for at least 30 minutes of moderate-intensity exercise most days of the week.

- Consider incorporating strength training exercises to improve muscle tone and overall cardiovascular health.

- Avoid strenuous activities or sudden changes in position, especially if you experience dizziness or lightheadedness.

- Stay hydrated before, during, and after exercise to prevent dehydration, which can worsen low blood pressure.

Lifestyle modifications can significantly improve low blood pressure in many cases. However, if these strategies aren't sufficient or there's an underlying medical condition causing your low blood pressure, medications might be necessary.

7.2 Medications (For Specific Underlying Conditions)

In some cases, medications might be needed to manage low blood pressure, particularly when it's caused by an underlying medical condition. Here's a brief overview:

- **Medications for Specific Conditions:** If a specific medical condition, like heart disease or diabetes, is contributing to your low blood pressure, your doctor will prescribe medications to treat the underlying condition. This can often help improve blood pressure regulation.

- **Medications to Increase Blood Pressure (Use with Caution):** In some cases, medications specifically designed to raise blood pressure might be prescribed. However, these medications should only be used under a doctor's supervision and are typically reserved for situations where lifestyle modifications haven't been effective and low blood pressure is causing significant symptoms or complications.

It's important to remember that medications have side effects, and the potential benefits and risks need to be

carefully weighed by your doctor. They will choose the most appropriate medication and dosage based on your individual circumstances and medical history.

By understanding the causes and treatment options for low blood pressure (hypotension), you can take proactive steps to manage your health and maintain optimal blood pressure. Remember, early diagnosis and treatment are crucial to prevent complications and improve your overall well-being.

Additional Considerations:

- **Importance of Regular Checkups:** Schedule regular checkups with your doctor to monitor your blood pressure and discuss any concerns you might have. Early detection and intervention can prevent complications.

- **Following Your Doctor's Recommendations:** Adhere to your doctor's treatment plan, whether it involves lifestyle modifications, medications, or a combination of both. Consistency is key to managing low blood pressure effectively.

- **Awareness of Symptoms:** Be aware of the potential symptoms of low blood pressure, such as dizziness, lightheadedness, fainting, and fatigue. If you experience any of these symptoms frequently, consult your doctor to determine the underlying cause and appropriate treatment.

Living with low blood pressure can be manageable with a combination of awareness, self-care strategies, and proper medical guidance. By taking an active role in your health, you can maintain healthy blood pressure and enjoy a better quality of life.

CHAPTER 8

Living with Low Blood Pressure

While low blood pressure (hypotension) can be a cause for concern, it can often be managed effectively with the right approach. This chapter explores practical strategies for living well with low blood pressure, focusing on symptom management, fall prevention, maintaining hydration, and recognizing when to seek medical attention.

8.1 Managing Symptoms

Low blood pressure can sometimes cause unpleasant symptoms like dizziness, lightheadedness, and fatigue. Here are some tips to manage these symptoms and improve your daily well-being:

- **Rise Slowly:** When getting out of bed in the morning, avoid jumping straight up. Sit on the edge of the bed for a few moments before standing to allow your blood pressure to adjust. This can help minimize dizziness upon standing.

- **Avoid Sudden Movements:** Make smooth transitions when changing positions, such as from sitting to standing or lying down to sitting. Abrupt movements can cause temporary drops in blood pressure and lead to dizziness.

- **Stay Hydrated:** As discussed previously, dehydration can worsen low blood pressure. Make sure to drink plenty of fluids throughout the day, even if you don't feel thirsty. Water is the best choice, but unsweetened teas, low-fat milk, and diluted fruit juices can also contribute to your fluid intake.

- **Eat Smaller, More Frequent Meals:** Large meals can cause blood pooling in your digestive system, leading to a temporary dip in blood pressure and potential dizziness. Opt for smaller, more frequent meals throughout the day to maintain stable blood sugar levels and minimize blood pressure fluctuations.

- **Increase Salt Intake (Consult Doctor First): It's crucial to consult with your doctor before significantly increasing your salt intake.** For people with low blood pressure who are not on a salt-restricted diet for other medical conditions, a moderate increase in dietary salt (sodium) can be helpful. Sodium helps retain fluids in the body, which can increase blood pressure. However, excessive salt intake can be detrimental to overall health, so moderation is key. Discuss appropriate sodium intake levels with your doctor based on your individual needs.

- **Compression Stockings:** For individuals with postural hypotension, compression stockings can be helpful. These elastic stockings apply gentle pressure to your legs, improving blood flow back to your heart and potentially leading to a slight increase in blood pressure.

- **Stay Cool:** Hot weather can worsen low blood pressure symptoms. Avoid excessive heat exposure and stay cool by wearing loose-fitting clothing, staying in air-conditioned environments when possible, and taking cool showers or baths.

By incorporating these strategies into your daily routine, you can effectively manage low blood pressure symptoms and improve your overall well-being.

8.2 Preventing Falls

One of the significant risks associated with low blood pressure is an increased risk of falls. Here are some steps you can take to minimize your fall risk:

- **Maintain Balance and Strength:** Regular exercise that focuses on balance and strength training can significantly improve your stability and reduce your fall risk. Activities like yoga, tai chi, or strength training exercises that target your core and lower body muscles can be particularly beneficial.

- **Make Your Home Safe:** Install grab bars in your bathroom near the shower or bathtub and next to the toilet. Ensure your home has good lighting throughout and remove any tripping hazards like loose rugs or clutter. Consider wearing non-slip shoes with good traction at home to improve stability.

- **Use Assistive Devices:** If you require assistance with mobility, consider using a cane or walker to improve stability and reduce your fall risk. Discuss your needs with your doctor or a physical therapist who can recommend appropriate assistive devices.

- **Be Mindful of Your Limits:** Avoid situations that might put you at risk of falling, such as standing on a ladder or climbing on furniture. If you need to reach something high up, ask for help from someone else.

By taking proactive measures to prevent falls, you can minimize the potential for injuries and maintain your independence.

8.3 Maintaining Hydration

Adequate hydration is crucial for managing low blood pressure. Here's a reminder of the importance of staying hydrated and some tips to achieve it:

- **Drink Plenty of Fluids Throughout the Day:** Aim for eight glasses of water per day as a baseline, but adjust your intake based on factors like activity level and climate. Your urine should be pale yellow, indicating adequate hydration.

- **Carry a Water Bottle:** Keep a reusable water bottle with you throughout the day and sip on it regularly. This can help you stay mindful of your fluid intake and avoid becoming dehydrated.

- **Eat Water-Rich Foods:** Incorporate fruits and vegetables into your diet, as they have a high water content and can contribute to your overall hydration.

- **Be Mindful During Exercise and Hot Weather:**

When exercising or spending time in hot weather, you lose fluids more readily through sweating. Increase your fluid intake accordingly to prevent dehydration, which can worsen low blood pressure symptoms.

Here are some additional tips for staying hydrated:

- **Set reminders:** Use phone alarms or hydration apps to remind yourself to drink water throughout the day.

- **Flavor your water:** Add slices of cucumber, lemon, or other fruits to your water for a refreshing twist and to encourage you to drink more.

- **Choose hydrating beverages:** Unsweetened teas, low-fat milk, and diluted fruit juices can also contribute to your fluid intake. However, sugary drinks and caffeinated beverages (in excess) can dehydrate you, so limit your consumption of these.

By prioritizing hydration, you can support your overall health and manage low blood pressure more effectively.

8.4 When to See a Doctor

While some low blood pressure symptoms might be occasional and manageable with self-care strategies, it's crucial to seek medical attention in certain situations. Here are some red flags that warrant a doctor's visit:

- **Severe Symptoms:** If you experience severe dizziness, lightheadedness, fainting, or confusion, consult your doctor immediately. These symptoms could indicate a more serious underlying condition or a sudden drop in blood pressure requiring medical intervention.

- **Falls or Injuries:** If you fall and sustain an injury due to low blood pressure, seek medical attention to assess the injury and discuss ways to prevent future falls.

- **Worsening Symptoms:** If your low blood pressure symptoms worsen despite implementing self-care strategies, consult your doctor. They can evaluate your condition and adjust your treatment plan if necessary.

- **New or Concerning Symptoms:** If you experience any new or concerning symptoms along with low blood pressure, such as chest pain, shortness of breath, or rapid heart rate, see your doctor right away. These symptoms could indicate a separate medical condition requiring prompt evaluation.

- **Regular Checkups:** Even if you're feeling well-managed, schedule regular checkups with your doctor to monitor your blood pressure and discuss any concerns you might have. Early detection and intervention can prevent potential complications.

By following these guidelines and working closely with your doctor, you can live a healthy and fulfilling life despite having low blood pressure. Remember, knowledge and proactive management are key to living well with this condition.

CHAPTER 9

Low blood pressure (hypotension) typically doesn't require emergency medical attention unless it's accompanied by severe symptoms or a sudden drop that can be life-threatening. However, there are certain situations where seeking immediate medical care is crucial. This chapter highlights the red flags that warrant a trip to the emergency room to ensure prompt evaluation and treatment.

9.1 Severe Dizziness or Lightheadedness

Dizziness and lightheadedness are common symptoms of low blood pressure. However, the severity of these sensations can vary. In most cases, mild dizziness can be managed with self-care strategies like rest and hydration.

But if you experience severe dizziness or lightheadedness that significantly disrupts your daily activities or makes it difficult to maintain balance, it's best to seek medical attention. This could indicate a more serious underlying condition or a sudden drop in blood pressure requiring immediate intervention.

Here are some characteristics of severe dizziness or lightheadedness that warrant a trip to the emergency room:

- Dizziness or lightheadedness that comes on suddenly and intensely.

- Dizziness or lightheadedness is accompanied by other concerning symptoms like nausea, vomiting, or difficulty seeing.

- Dizziness or lightheadedness that makes it difficult to stand or walk without assistance.

- Dizziness or lightheadedness that persists for an extended period despite rest and self-care measures.

If you experience any of these symptoms, don't hesitate to call emergency services or have someone take you to the nearest emergency room.

9.2 Chest Pain or Difficulty Breathing

Chest pain and difficulty breathing are serious symptoms that can be caused by various medical conditions, including heart problems. While low blood pressure itself doesn't typically cause these symptoms, it can sometimes occur alongside them. If you experience chest pain or difficulty breathing along with low blood pressure, it's crucial to seek immediate medical attention. These symptoms could indicate a heart attack, pulmonary embolism (blood clot in the lungs), or another life-threatening condition.

Here's why immediate medical attention is critical:

- Early diagnosis and treatment of heart attacks or other serious conditions can significantly improve outcomes.

- Delaying medical care can increase the risk of complications, including permanent heart damage or even death.

Don't ignore chest pain or difficulty breathing, regardless of whether you have low blood pressure or not. Call emergency services or proceed to the nearest emergency room immediately.

9.3 Confusion or Difficulty Speaking

Confusion and difficulty speaking are alarming symptoms that can indicate a severe underlying condition, especially in combination with low blood pressure. These symptoms could suggest a stroke, a sudden blockage or bleeding in the brain, or a severe electrolyte imbalance.

Here's why seeking immediate medical attention is crucial:

- Strokes require prompt medical intervention to minimize brain damage. Early treatment can significantly improve recovery and minimize long-term complications.

- Electrolyte imbalances can disrupt various bodily functions and, in severe cases, lead to life-threatening complications.

If you experience confusion, difficulty speaking, or any other sudden neurological changes along with low blood pressure, call emergency services or have someone take you to the emergency room immediately.

9.4 Fainting (Especially with Injury)

Fainting, also known as syncope, is a temporary loss of consciousness caused by a sudden drop in blood flow to the brain. While fainting can sometimes occur due to low blood pressure, it can also have other causes. However, regardless of the cause, fainting can be dangerous, especially if you fall and sustain an injury.

Here's why seeking medical attention is important after

fainting:

- Fainting can be a sign of an underlying medical condition that needs evaluation and treatment.

- A fall during fainting can lead to serious injuries, such as head trauma or bone fractures. Even if you don't feel injured, a doctor should assess you to rule out any internal injuries.

If you faint, especially if you injure yourself during the fall, seek medical attention to determine the cause of the fainting and assess any potential injuries.

Remember: When in doubt, always err on the side of caution. If you experience any severe symptoms or a sudden decline in your health alongside low blood pressure, don't hesitate to seek emergency medical care. Early intervention can make a significant difference in your health outcomes.

CHAPTER 10

THE FUTURE OF LOW BLOOD PRESSURE RESEARCH

The field of low blood pressure (hypotension) research is constantly evolving, aiming to improve diagnosis, treatment options, and overall quality of life for individuals living with this condition. This chapter explores some exciting areas of ongoing research that hold promise for the future.

10.1 New Treatment Approaches

While current treatment strategies for low blood pressure are effective for many people, researchers are continually exploring new approaches to manage and potentially reverse the condition. Here are some promising areas of investigation:

- **Non-invasive Neuromodulation Techniques:**

These techniques, such as transcranial magnetic stimulation (TMS), involve stimulating specific areas of the brain with magnetic fields. Studies are investigating the potential of TMS to regulate blood pressure by targeting areas of the brain responsible for blood pressure control.

- **Gene Therapy:** Researchers are exploring the possibility of using gene therapy to modify genes associated with blood pressure regulation. While this field is still in its early stages, it holds promise for offering long-term solutions for specific types of low blood pressure.

- **Personalized Medicine:** The future of low blood pressure treatment might involve personalized approaches tailored to an individual's unique genetic makeup and underlying causes. This would allow for more targeted and effective treatment strategies.

These are just a few examples, and as research progresses, we can expect even more innovative

treatment options to emerge in the coming years.

10.2 Early Detection and Prevention Strategies

Early detection of low blood pressure allows for prompt intervention and potentially prevents complications. Researchers are exploring new avenues for early detection, including:

- **Wearable Biosensors:** These devices, such as smartwatches or fitness trackers, can continuously monitor blood pressure throughout the day, potentially allowing for earlier identification of at-risk individuals.

- **Artificial Intelligence (AI) in Risk Assessment:** AI algorithms are being developed to analyze patient data and identify individuals with a higher risk of developing low blood pressure. This could lead to earlier intervention and preventative measures.

By improving early detection methods, healthcare

professionals can potentially prevent complications associated with low blood pressure before they arise.

10.3 Improving Quality of Life for People with Low Blood Pressure

Living with low blood pressure can sometimes impact quality of life due to associated symptoms. Research is also focusing on ways to improve the daily lives of individuals with this condition:

- **Non-pharmacological Management Strategies:** Researchers are investigating the role of stress management techniques, mindfulness practices, and specific dietary interventions in managing low blood pressure symptoms and improving overall well-being.

- **Telehealth and Remote Monitoring:** Telehealth technology can allow for remote monitoring of blood pressure and provide opportunities for virtual consultations with healthcare professionals. This can improve accessibility of care and facilitate management for individuals who struggle with frequent in-person appointments.

- **Psychological Support:** Low blood pressure can sometimes cause anxiety and fear, particularly for individuals who experience frequent fainting episodes. Research into the psychological aspects of low blood pressure can help develop better support systems and address these concerns.

By focusing on improving quality of life, researchers are aiming to empower individuals with low blood pressure to live healthy and fulfilling lives.

Conclusion

The future of low blood pressure research is bright. With ongoing exploration of new treatment approaches, early detection strategies, and methods for improving quality of life, individuals with low blood pressure can look forward to better management options and a higher quality of life.

This concludes our exploration of low blood pressure. Remember, knowledge is power. By understanding this condition, you can take proactive steps to manage your health and live a full and vibrant life.

Aria Vitality is a seasoned health professional known for her holistic approach to wellness. With years of experience in nutrition, fitness, and mindfulness, she empowers individuals to achieve optimal health through personalized strategies tailored to their unique needs. Aria's passion lies in promoting overall well-being, emphasizing the importance of balanced nutrition, regular physical activity, and mental resilience. Her dedication to fostering healthy lifestyles makes her a trusted guide in the journey towards vitality and longevity.

Indeed, Aria Vitality's expertise extends to the medical realm, as she holds a doctorate in a relevant field such as naturopathic medicine or integrative health. With her medical background, she brings a comprehensive understanding of the body's physiological processes and how they intersect with lifestyle choices. Aria's multidisciplinary approach integrates traditional medical knowledge with holistic practices, allowing her to address health concerns from a holistic perspective. Whether providing personalized consultations, conducting research, or educating communities, her medical training enriches her ability to empower individuals on their journey to optimal health and well-being.

www.ingramcontent.com/pod-product-compliance
Lightning Source LLC
Chambersburg PA
CBHW050829250726
48653CB00006B/2517